THE

MAYPOLE

MANUAL

Mike Ruff & Jenny Read

www.themaypolemanual.co.uk

A Spinningpath MUSIC book

Spinningpath MUSIC

9 Park Street, Crediton, Devon, EX17 3HL

Copyright© Mike Ruff and Jenny Read, 2014

First published in Great Britain in 2014 by Spinningpath MUSIC

The information in this book is meant to supplement, not replace, proper dance training. Like any physical activity involving speed, equipment, balance and environmental factors, maypole dancing poses some inherent risk. The authors and publisher advise readers to take full responsibility for their safety and know their limits, and the limits of the participants. Before practising the skills described in this book, be sure that your equipment is well maintained, and do not take risks beyond your level of experience, aptitude, training, and comfort level.

British Library Cataloguing in Publication Data

Data Available

ISBN 978-0-9572846-1-6

3 5 7 9 10 8 6 4 2

All photographs and diagrams are copyright.
Details of copyright holders are available on request.

Cover illustration by Claire Mokrauer-Madden

Book design, production and editing by Jenny Read & Mike Ruff

Photography by Robert Darch, Tim Seelig, Claire Mokrauer-Madden,
Ann Wise and Tony Rundle

Images used by kind permission of Starcross Primary School,
Spinningpath Arts CIC and Bowland Academy

Diagrams by Mo Pietroni

Music setting by Chris Haigh and Ed Rennie

Printed by Beaver Reprographics

We have attempted to trace the true owner of the copyright of all images which appear in this book. Should we have been guilty of error or omission please inform us and we will amend future copies and post the appropriate credit on the Maypole Manual website.

Why Maypole?

Enjoyment

The best reason we know for Maypole Dancing is that it is fun to do, great for all ages and abilities, and visually pleasing for those watching. People enjoy trying the dances and the teacher's job becomes one of harnessing enthusiasm. Learning takes place automatically and teamwork becomes instinctive as the dancers realise that they have to work together to get results. While many people think that Maypole is just for children, most adults love to have a go!

Three Dimensions

Because a Maypole is a three dimensional tool, it takes learning into a different environment and dancers get a chance to think and learn in new and creative ways. It is also one of the few forms of dance where the focus is not on the dancers but on the patterns and the ribbons, and the dances can be adapted to suit the abilities and fitness of the group.

A Cross - Curricular Tool

The various cross curricular links are dealt with elsewhere and the more confident the teachers become the more this will happen naturally as everyone is likely to want to explore new ideas as they arise.

Cultural Heritage

We start from the point of Maypoles being part of our cultural heritage but that this is shared. The Maypole is not unique to England and similar activities can be found around the globe. Even more common is the idea of seasonal celebrations so that once again the Maypole becomes the starting point rather than the end product.

Introducing Music and Dance

Our own interests lie with traditional music and dance and we have found that once Maypole Dancing has been introduced then exploring different dance forms and musical styles can become much easier.

A Visual Artform

Because the Maypole can be seen, it can easily become the focus of activities at summer fetes and the like, and including Maypole Dancing in these events then becomes a tradition. Better still, because it is so visible and relatively cheap compared to other pieces of equipment, raising funds for a new Maypole or to enhance the existing tradition becomes much easier for any school or group.

Contents

NOTES FOR TEACHERS

RIBBON DANCES

The *Maypole Manual Music* CD can be purchased via our website: *www.themaypolemanual.co.uk*

Acknowledgements

This book has been a long time in the making, and we owe huge thanks to all the people who have helped it to reach print. Thank you to our family and friends for endless patience with all things maypole related! Thank you Tamsin and Ruth for sharing your teaching expertise. Thanks to Quicksilver for an amazing CD to dance to, and Alan for your help with printing. Thanks to all at Tradamis and Spinningpath Arts CIC for supporting this new project, and to everyone who has proofread or commented on sections of the book before going to press.

About the Authors

Mike Ruff gave up any attempt at a day job more than 20 years ago to concentrate on being a musician. Working in schools came a few years later and the purchase of a Maypole meant "have Maypole will travel" has become a major part of Mike's work ever since. He has taught dancers of all ages and abilities, creating shows and teaching teachers. In 2012, he worked with the English National Ballet to provide Maypole dancing and music for morris dancing for their *Big Dance* event.

Two creative partnership projects in Slough in 2002 resulted in Mike forming Tradamis which is now a charity, with Mike as Director and one of the Trustees. Through a nationwide network of practitioners, Tradamis offers a wide range of teaching modules, training, mentoring, and resources on traditional and historical dance and music aimed at increasing appreciation of our cultural heritage as widely as possible.

Mike's work as a musician continues alongside his educational work. In addition to his band *Quicksilver*, who you will hear on the CD, he performs Victorian Music Hall with *Allcock and Brown* and, as a Tudor minstrel, with *Bag o'Peas*. Add in a wide range of solo activities and a series of talks on the history of dancing, and there is a whole separate, and occasionally overlapping, career which takes him from village greens and museums to the streets of London and Wembley Stadium.

Jenny Read is a freelance music and dance teacher with years of experience in folk and community arts. Having gained her BA Hons degree in Music, she worked as an instrumental music teacher, community worker, and carer for adults with learning difficulties and autism. Her lifelong interest in dance became more than a hobby when she established a local youth dance team which went on to perform at festivals and events across the country.

Following a growing number of requests to teach dance at various schools and events, Jenny trained at the Trinity Laban Conservatoire of Music and Dance, becoming the first folk dance artist to gain the Level 6 Diploma in Dance Teaching and Learning for Children and Young People from Trinity College London. She now runs regular dance classes, Early Years' music and movement sessions, musicianship training and continues to work as a freelance instrumental teacher. Jenny is a director of the new Devon-based folk arts social enterprise, *Spinningpath Arts CIC*, taking folk arts into schools and community settings.

As a performer, she dances and sings with the UK's old-time American string band, *The Buffalo Gals*, plays the piano for the Devon-based English ceilidh band, *A New Vintage*, and leads workshops and performances with her percussive dance team, *Appakella*. She is also three times winner of the Dartmoor Step Dance Competition.

Foreword

This book started as a series of notes four years ago for a Tradamis Training Workshop that Mike was running. It was clear then that there was enough about each dance to create a book; something that gives all the tricks for teaching, the hints and the pitfalls inherent in the dances and something that does not require an expert to get you started. Others agreed and here it is.

In 2012 there was another teacher training session planned in Devon. Mike could not do it but Jenny could and the collaboration was born. Jenny's more formal training as a teacher, dancer and musician has given a whole new dimension to the book that might otherwise have been missing.

Music is essential for Maypole and this project needed a new CD to accompany the dances. This is just the sort of challenge that Mike's band, Quicksilver, enjoys and we had a lot of fun putting it together. If you haven't already purchased a copy of the CD, you will find them on our website: *www.themaypolemanual.co.uk* .

Finally, what should be included? We hope that there is all the basic information and a bit more. The classic John Ruskin dances and their links to Victorian Society had to be included. Then the new dances and our creative approach will open up Maypole Dancing to many, both younger and older, allowing everyone much more scope. Looking further back in time there are some genuine Tudor dances which work incredibly well around a Maypole and link it to another key section of the history curriculum. All of that brings us to 21 dances but Mike's original list had another 14 rarely used dances and we have already had suggestions for others.

This is where modern technology helps out. The website *(www.themaypolemanual.co.uk)* is a vital part of this project, with links to other projects, new dances and video clips of what people are doing. We will be adding details and updates that are not in the book to download, ideas for other dances and information on other products.

At the end of it all we hope that you will share the joy that we have had from dancing and teaching Maypole Dancing. For Mike it started as a simple set of requests:

- Can you play for Maypole Dancing? He could.
- Where do we get one? He found out and bought one.
- How do we do the dances? He looked some up and started from there.
- Can we try out some new ideas? Most certainly!

Enjoy!

Mike & Jenny

Origins and History of Maypole Dancing

Early Maypoles

It is thought that the earliest Maypoles formed part of a celebration of Summer. They were probably linked with mystical beliefs such as tree worship, but also provided opportunities to dance and have a good time. They were almost certainly simple trees cut down and re-erected in the centre of a village green. Illustration show that, by the 16th and 17th centuries, Maypoles were often very tall. Although actual dances were not recorded, the Puritans, who hated Maypoles and all they signified, have helped our knowledge by describing in great detail what they were destroying!

Is this one of the earliest Maypole illustrations?

No ribbons

After the Restoration, many Maypoles were re-instated. One of the most notable stood in the Strand at an impressive 134 feet tall (approx. 41m)... until Sir Isaac Newton used parts of it as a base for his telescope! Some of the maypoles from that period still survive in villages around the country. None of them had ribbons; not only were the poles so tall that it would be impractical, but machines for making ribbons were not invented until 1858. This would mean that any ribbons before then would have been extremely difficult and expensive to make. It is reasonable to assume that Maypole Dances were simply any that were popular at the time, either country dances or morris dancing of some sort.

It is also likely that circle dances would have been used when space allowed. We have included some of these dances, not just to reflect the history, but because experience tells us that they enhance any performance.

John Ruskin and the English Tradition

The Maypole Dancing that most people think of was introduced by John Ruskin to Whitelands College in 1881, creating a sequence of dances and a May Pageant which generations of teachers learnt and took with them wherever they went on to teach. By the middle of the 20th century, Maypole Dancing had become a major tradition, much of which survives to the present day.

Maypoles around the world

While Maypoles are regarded as something very English, they exist in many other parts of the world, although sometimes in slightly different forms. Pictures from Germany show Maypoles with ribbons, and versions of these dances still exist in Brazil and Argentina. Illustrations from the French Court of Louis XIV show Maypoles as part of their large scale entertainments, and other traditions are found in Galicia (Spain), Finland & Mexico.

We also know of people who learnt Maypole Dancing sixty or more years ago in Jamaica, Trinidad and elsewhere in the Caribbean. While they may have started from Whitelands College a century ago, these dances have certainly taken on a life of their own. Interestingly, in other parts of the world it is often the adults that do the Maypole Dances and it does seem as though the idea of it being something just for children is uniquely English.

Maypole Dancing for the Coronation of George V in 1911. Note the use of recorded music - its nothing new!

New ideas

Fortunately, after a period of decline, Maypole Dancing is experiencing a revival due to a greater awareness of our own culture, and the sheer enjoyment of dancers and audience alike. The main difference is that there is now a far greater degree of creativity, with new dances and styles being invented all the time. Quite often the same ideas will be repeated, but that does not necessarily mean they have been copied. Variations occur as dancers try out new ideas, influenced by popular dance styles and music.

Costume

Originally, dancers would have worn their best clothes. However, by the Victorian period there was a deliberate attempt to re-create an image of "Merrie England" (which disputedly never existed) with costumes being chosen to reflect that.

Nowadays anything goes. There are Tudor Peasants, Victorian Ladies and Gentlemen, Medieval Costumes (which can be quite grand), sports kit, simple variations on school uniform or just sashes to identify dancers from spectators.

Music

In the early days, music would have been played on instruments such as the pipe and tabor or the English bagpipes. By the time of John Ruskin, the concertina or fiddle would have been added, with later instruments including the accordion, flute and any others loud enough to carry in the open air. Whilst this still holds true, people will now often dance to recordings, whether that be traditional country dance music similar to the above, or more modern pop songs and rap.

St George's Kermis with the Dance Around the Maypole; Pieter Breughel the Younger, 1627

No ribbons, but clearly a lot of fun!

Setting up the Maypole

The following instructions are for an *Educational Aids* Maypole* or similar. However, many of the principles, such as the distribution of ribbons, will be the same for most maypoles. Most of the set-up can be done by one person, but steps 4 and 5 are easier with an extra pair of hands to help with the lifting.

1. Place the upper section of the pole in the base and fix the crown on top;

2. Use the bolt to stop the inner ring from rotating. (We only know of one dance, The Waterwheel, where both rings need to rotate freely);

3. Place two colours of ribbons alternately around the inner ring, e.g. yellow and green;

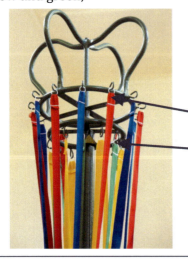

4. Then add the other two colours, in this case red and blue, to the outer ring;

5. Now lift the upper section of pole, the crown and ribbons clear of the base;

6. Place the lower section of pole into the base and lift the rest onto the top;

7. Tighten the securing bolts at the base and you are ready for action.

Outer Ring: Red & Blue

Inner Ring: Green & Yellow

The Educational Aids Maypole has been designed for maximum stability. Since these photographs were taken, additional weight has been added for maximum functionality and stability. These maypoles are easy to transport and can be stored in a surprisingly small space. Other manufacturers have taken a different approach, and adjustments may have to be made to the dancing as they would for dancing with an older maypole. Some other maypoles rely on non-dancers to keep the pole stable or need to be placed in a hole in the ground; great for stability but not always easily assembled for a quick practice.

How many ribbons?

Obviously this will depend on how many dancers you have. The pole has hooks for 24 ribbons, so 24 dancers are ideal. If working with a larger group, then having people sitting out and changing in after each dance works very well. Reserves are essential for any dance performance, and those spare dancers can be used to hand out ribbons or to be extra ballast for the Maypole.

When working with younger children, there is a benefit to having 2 children per ribbon where possible, so you may prefer to have them all up and dancing rather than swapping them on and off the 'subs bench'.

Too many dancers?

See our suggestions for dealing with this on *p22*. For other ideas, see the *Inclusion* section on *p12-14*.

Should you have less than 24 dancers, then things become slightly more complex. Many of the dances, but not all, work best with an even number of dancers, and a lot require equal numbers of the different colours so we generally try and reduce the number of ribbons to suit this. We rarely use 20 ribbons but jump to 16 or 12. Most dances work with 8 ribbons, but the results are generally less satisfactory.

Working with fewer ribbons

When working with 8 or 12 ribbons, it is logical to space them out evenly, either by missing every other hook, or missing 2 out of 3 respectively, but still keeping the same sequence of colours. With 16 ribbons, the trick is to miss 1 hook in 3, giving a sequence of red, blue, miss one, red, blue, miss one, for example.

It is best not to leave ribbons dangling as they can spoil the look of the dance and generally get in the way. To adjust the number of ribbons on the crown, you may need help to lift the upper section down and back up again.

Chrysanthemum for 12 - a minimalist effect...

Indoors or outdoors?

See *p65* for some practical considerations.

What should we wear?

Schools and groups generally have a policy on what to wear for physical activities, so just combine this with common sense! All we ask for is suitable footwear (plimsolls or trainers) and clothes that are comfortable to move in. Whether this is school uniform or PE kit really just depends on the length of the session and the level of energy you expect of your group. Bare feet are also fine as long as the dancers do not kick the base but, if the final performance is likely to be outside, it is better to practise in shoes from the outset.

Inclusion

We all want everyone to be included in the dance, but there are a range of reasons why this may seem difficult. Apart from physical limitations, some dancers may have language difficulties, sensory disorders, social or behavioural needs. Some may find noise and movement overwhelming, or find it hard to orient themselves spatially. The good news is that the most successful means of addressing these needs are often to the benefit of the whole group, enriching the experience of learning for everyone. Here is a list of strategies, interventions and adaptations that we have tried and found to be successful in the context of maypole dancing. We are sure there are many more!

Clear expectations

Some people feel very anxious in a new setting. It can be helpful to spend a little time before the session working through the process of learning a group dance and what will be expected of them. Mistakes are bound to happen - they are a normal part of learning something new - but the group will work together to make the pattern successfully.

Slow it down

If a dancer has mobility issues and needs longer to execute a figure, simply double or quadruple the length of phrase being used. Remind the group that they are part of a team, and that rushing ahead or overtaking will only spoil the pattern. They need to pull together and make sure that everyone moves at the same speed.

Buddying

Pairing up dancers with a strong partner, or *buddying*, can help to give physical support and guidance, as well as helping with spatial orientation. If you are working with very young children, it can be really helpful to pair them with children from an older class. Some dancers seem to instinctively give a firm yet gentle lead to their partner, but others need help to do this effectively and safely. They may also need help in working out how to share the ribbon, rather than one taking it over from the other. Bear in mind, when choosing partners for buddying, that dancers with hypersensitivity can find touch difficult or even painful.

Position your dancers

Identify the points in the dance that might be disorientating and seek to place reliable dancers nearby who are able to give a strong lead. Depending on the dance, these dancers may need to take up adjacent ribbons, or other ribbons of the same colour.

In Twister, pairing younger and older dancers across the circle gives a strong lead for each couple.

Quality not quantity

Being in a noisy, moving environment can be overwhelming for someone with impaired hearing or heightened sensitivity, for example dancers with autistic spectrum disorders. Using a good quality PA system will provide clear musical quality, which will be far easier to work with than the distortion resulting from a small CD player turned up too loud.

Activity

Working with the music at a lower volume can encourage dancers to listen more carefully, often resulting in them being more aware and in time. You can even turn it into a game:

Start the dance with everyone stepping in time to the music at your normal volume. Turn it down and down – can they still keep in time? Can they maintain the pulse while you fade the music out altogether? Can they find the beat again when you fade the music back in?

Being able to work with music of a better quality, but at a lower volume, can greatly reduce stress, whilst helping the group to become more aware of the music they are dancing to. For dancers with very limited hearing, visual stimulus is also vital: set a good clear tempo with a visual count-in, and show this pulse through your body language as the dance continues.

Use clear language

Even for students with a good grasp of everyday English, the terms used in dance may be unfamiliar and need clarification. Familiarise yourself with both the tune and the dance, and practise calling each move before the end of a phrase so that dancers have time to hear and process the call with enough time to act on it at the start of the next phrase. Not only will the dancers benefit from the clear instructions, but it will make you a better dance caller too!

Be creative

Think about different ways to present the same information. For example, as well as saying 'blue', hold up a blue card (or toy!) as a visual cue for the dancers holding blue ribbons to move. If you have more dancers than ribbons, this is a great job to delegate, since it engages them actively, not only in the process of the dance, but in learning to think ahead to help the other dancers.

Less people moving at once

Simply reducing the number of ribbons will give the dancers more room to move, which can be helpful for people with mobility issues or who struggle with busy, moving environments.

Cobweb for 12 - more room to manoeuvre.

Alternatively, choose a dance where only some of the dancers move at once e.g. The Chrysanthemum (each colour in turn). If you need to simplify things even further, don't be afraid to experiment with having even fewer dancers moving at a time. For example, Silkstream can be easily adapted so that each pair creates their plait independently, before parading as a group. Experiment—you might even create a new dance in the process!

All change

You may need to enable a dancer to leave the dance at some point, perhaps due to a physical condition or heightened anxiety. In order for this to happen with minimal disruption, it can be helpful to have an agreed signal from the dancer that they wish to leave, and to have a capable replacement able to step in quickly to continue the dance in their position. In fact, this makes a great game for the whole group to try!

Activity

Have a line of dancers ready to step into the dance. Tell the dancers that, if they want to swap out of the dance, all they need to do is to raise their hand, and someone will appear to take their place. The main rule? Don't let go of your ribbon until you have handed it safely to someone else! How long can they keep the dance going? Can the 'subs' pick up the dance in their new position?

Additional benefits of this game are that dancers develop an understanding of the dance as a whole, and have a lot of fun working together to keep it moving. If you find yourself with extra dancers in a performance, it can make the 'subs' bench a much more purposeful place to be.

Some practical adaptations for wheelchair users

Dancers in wheelchairs are able to move at great speed and with careful control. But this usually requires the use of both hands, which makes it difficult to hold the ribbon. One very practical solution is to create a mast for the wheelchair using something strong, light and flexible, such as the carbon fibre rods used for making kites. With a loop of wire (from a coat hanger, for example) attached to one end, it can be taped to the back of the wheelchair using "gaffer" or "duct" tape. It is then possible to attach the loop of the ribbon to the loop in the mast so that the ribbon is approximately the same height as the ribbons held by the standing dancers, leaving hands free for manipulating the wheelchair.

Clearly certain dances will work better than others, and having 12 ribbons rather than 24 can allow more room to manoeuvre. Using this method it has been possible to include up to 3 wheelchair users in a single dance, and we can't see any reason why this shouldn't be more.

Think ahead to the performance

Change can be difficult and confusing. It may not be practical to rehearse in the same space as the performance will occur, but there are many other factors that you can consider in order to build in as much consistency as possible from the outset: ribbon colour, position and orientation of the group, neighbouring dancers and the instructional language used. The more familiar the performance situation, the less stressful it will be for everyone!

Above all, help your dancers to understand that they are part of a team. Whatever their role, each of them has an important part to play.

Keeping it relevant: links to the curriculum

Wherever you teach, the curriculum keeps on changing, making it difficult to offer specific links for those teaching maypole in educational settings. However, Maypole Dancing is a rich tradition which can open all sorts of lines of enquiry for the active learner across a range of subjects. What follows is simply a selection of ideas to get you, and your dancers, thinking. Further links and curriculum updates will be available on our website *(www.themaypolemanual.co.uk)* and we welcome input from teachers on this.

Language skills

1. Speaking & listening

Maypole dancers need to listen and respond to direct verbal instructions. Beyond this, there is plenty of scope for discussion before, during or after a session when students can think about elements of the dance, context and process:

- What worked well?

- How could we improve our performance?

- What happens if we dance to different music? How does our dancing change?

Thinking ahead to the performance, could someone prepare an introduction to the dance, giving them an opportunity to speak in front of an audience?

2. Reading & writing

Maypole dances follow very simple instructions, which rely on the correct ordering of colours to create the patterns. This offers an ideal opportunity for pupils to:

- Write their own instructions for a dance they know

- Follow a set of instructions e.g. the 'dance at a glance' box, or instructions written by one of their peers

- Create their own dances and write instructions for others to follow

Of course, this is particularly useful in a class context as a way of engaging children who are not dancing. The complexity of instruction can be varied according to the age and ability of the students.

Children can also be encouraged to research and present aspects of the history and context of Maypole dancing, and other related traditional dance forms such as English country dance, Tudor circle dances and circle dances from other cultures. Writing an introductory text for the performance can develop a child's use of descriptive language and delivery of the key facts.

Science

As with any physical activity, dance can be used to explore elements of science:

- Speed of motion, e.g. faster, slower

- Direction and changes of direction

- Heart-rate and understanding of the body

It is also a great forum for tackling problems as a group, testing and refining solutions.

Art, design & technology

So many choices, it just depends how creative you want to get...! For starters, why not think about the following?

- The working characteristics of a maypole

e.g. wheels, joints that allow movement

- Plaiting, weaving and other ways of making patterns and cloth from separate strands

- Make a 2 or 3-D model of a working maypole, reflecting on design, variations and modifications

Sport & P.E.

Maypole Dancing obviously ticks this box because of its very nature, but is there more to it than that? Yes, of course! Maypole Dancing is not just about learning prescribed sequences, but about being creative with the dance as a whole and developing core skills as individuals. Warm-up activities offer a fun forum for exploring different ways to travel whilst developing children's sense of spatial awareness necessary for the dances. As the children dance, encourage them to think about the following aspects which are fundamental to dance technique in a range of styles:

- Changes of speed, direction and level

- Balance and control of one's own body

- Awareness of the other dancers in the space

- Evaluating and improving one's own performance

History & Geography

Maypole is a great catalyst for thinking about changes in community life, locally, nationally and globally, and exploring how traditions have been carried from one community to another.

- How is social dance different today?

- Why did some traditions die out, and some remain?

- Why are traditions being revived today?

- Where traditions have continued, why and how has this happened?

Delve deeper into the reasons why people dance, and why it is important in community and social life.

Music

Is the music just there to dance to, or can you learn more about it as you go? Depending on their age and musical awareness, encourage the children to:

Identify the instruments on the CD: What do they hear playing? Which families of instruments do they belong to?

Compare and contrast 2 tracks on the CD: Can they find the beat? Which one is faster? Can they clap the rhythm? Can they sing the melody? Which words could they use to describe the music?

Play along: Even the youngest child enjoys banging a drum along with these tunes. More experienced musicians may be able to play the tune on their instrument (see the sheet music provided), or pick out the chords on a guitar. If you have a school band, why not get them to accompany your performance?

Think about the structure of the music, and how they can tell the difference between the sections.

Think about the factors that make this music good for dancing to. Why else do people make music, and how does it fulfill different purposes?

ICT

By all means use computers to research and document Maypole-related projects.. But think outside the box too... The use of digital cameras, for example, provides an amazing opportunity for dancers to record and reflect on their work. What worked well about their performance? How could they improve it next time?

So, if all this isn't enough, let's have a quick think about how Maypole Dancing ties in with the broader curriculum of active learning and citizenship.

Thinking skills

As with any subject, the more you can make Maypole learning an interactive experience, the more your students will develop their skills of information processing, reasoning, enquiry, creative thinking and evaluation.

Team work & social skills

Nobody can create a maypole dance on their own. With minimal contact and conversation, dancers need to work together to create the pattern. Can they take responsibility for themselves, deal with mistakes and contribute in positive ways to improving the end product without pointing the finger at other people?

Cultural

We have heard from a number of local teachers that, while their students have a healthy respect for cultures across the globe, they have little experience of their own cultural heritage. At a recent training session, two teachers were reminiscing about their time as pupils at that school, and how the high street used to be closed for the annual May Day celebrations at which they danced. They were really excited about getting the children in school dancing again, even though they didn't think that closing the high street would be likely! May Day celebrations, summer fetes... Maypole Dancing can help to create a sense of community by giving participants a shared experience, and drawing in the wider community to enjoy the event. Some of our more enterprising children are also using dance to raise money for charity, which opens up even more areas for learning and growing!

Towards a sustainable future

So much of our entertainment is loud and fast and reliant on technology. This is all well and good, but sometimes children need help to experience activities that are slower, quieter, and more connected to the seasons of the year. Maypole Dancing is a great way of doing this. If you can find a good musician, you could even opt for a low carbon performance without amplification!

"From the standpoint of young learners, making links between subjects enriches and enlivens them..." Sir Jim Rose CBE, Review of the Primary Curriculum, 2009

http://www.educationengland.org.uk/documents/pdfs/2009-IRPC-final-report.pdf

Warming up

Maypole dancing may look fairly gentle but, as with any physical activity, it is important to warm up and cool down properly. You will want to focus mainly on the legs and arms, but it is also a good opportunity to increase the core strength of the dancers. Here are a few fun and simple activities which are good for warming up and embedding techniques which will be useful later in the session:

Homing pigeons

Raises pulse and develops spatial awareness. Enables dancers to return confidently to their starting positions without colliding with other dancers!

Standing in a circle (best done without the maypole in the centre) or simply scattered around the room, ask dancers to look carefully at their place and memorise important features e.g. the person to either side of them, marks on the floor, on the wall etc. Name the dancers 'red', 'green', 'yellow' & 'blue' around the room. Choose one group to move around the room and then, on your signal (a clap or whistle), to move back as quickly as possible to their starting place. Repeat with the other groups one at a time. As their spatial awareness develops, you may ask more than one group to move together, watching out for other dancers as they go. A fun addition is to

think about different ways of travelling e.g. skipping, crawling, moving sideways – maybe they can come up with their own ideas....?

Copycat

Develops awareness of other dancers, posture and isolation of movement: depending on the actions you choose, this can be used for mobilisation of joints and/or stretches.

Ask the dancers to spread out around the room and face the teacher. Find a good, tall standing position, feet under hips, backs straight. Tell them that you will do a series of actions, which they need to copy as precisely as possible. Concentrate on leg and arm movements, starting small and getting larger.

If you use this exercise over a number of sessions, you can develop their skills by splitting them into pairs, facing each other as if looking in a mirror. Their task is to copy as closely as possible, but without touching. At your signal, dancers swap who is leading and who is following.

Try scattering the pairs around the room, with the dancers as far away from their partners as possible. Can they still copy precisely from a distance, without being distracted by other dancers? At your signal, swap who is taking the lead.

Opposites

Develops awareness of other dancers, posture and isolation of movement: depending on the actions you choose, this can be used for mobilisation of joints and/or stretches. It is also a fun way to prepare for version 3 of the Single Plait.

As with Copycat, ask the dancers to spread out around the room, facing the teacher. But this time, whatever the teacher does, the dancers must do the opposite. If the teacher puts their arms up, then dancers put their arms down. If the teacher stretches out 'big', the dancers curl up 'small'. If the teacher leans up and to the right, they lean down and to the left etc... As a progression, dancers can work in pairs as for Copycat.

Cooling down

The simplest way to cool down is to do a reverse of your warm-ups, stretching, mobilising (to release the build up of lactic acid in the muscles) and bringing the pulse rate back down. Any of the above exercises can be used to this effect, if done in a calm way: gentle music can help.

Copycat: How closely can a dancer follow their partner?

Music for dancing

The music is a vital part of any dance, and Maypole Dancing is no exception. Your choice of music can radically change the style and character of the dance, whether it is live or recorded. Here are some factors to consider:

Live or recorded?

Live music is great to dance to as the musicians can respond to the dancers and vice versa, and it really enhances any event. John Ruskin put together a sequence of tunes for his dances that were published by Curwen and regarded as the definitive tunes. However, unless recreating a John Ruskin show, there is no need to use them and they are out of print anyhow. Instead, we have included a selection of tunes at the back of this book which your musicians might like to try. Having said that, folk music is a living tradition, and we would encourage you to experiment with whatever music you like: anything from the traditional style through to Drum n' Bass, Rap and Pop songs. After all, many of the dances in this book are quite recent, so why shouldn't the music be the same? Often people find it more practical to dance to recorded music, and it does open up a range of stylistic options. Whichever you choose, feel free to experiment. By using different music for Maypole Dancing, it can encourage greater interest in the music and maybe even our indigenous culture.

The Quicksilver CD

The CD that accompanies this book (available separately from *www.themaypolemanual.co.uk*) is an echo of some of the most successful tracks that we have used in the past. So as well as English and Celtic Folk influences you will find bits of Jazz, Swing, Rock and Early Music. While we have given suggestions for which tracks work with each dance, you might find that you prefer to use others.

We hope that you will find the new CD good to dance to, lively, interesting and suitably varied but we will list other music that people find useful on the website, along with new tracks to download if there is the demand. If you have musicians around they may also want to play some of the tunes and we have included nine of them *(see p62-64)* with chords for this purpose.

Using different music

If you want to use your own music, what do you need to think about? It needs to have:

- A strong pulse;

- A good tempo;

- Regular phrases (though not necessarily if your dancers are confident at responding to other cues e.g. lyrics or verse/chorus structures).

Above all, it needs to be danceable! Certain rhythms will work better for skipping or walking, so bear this in mind when making your selection.

It can also be fun to try dancing the same dance to a totally different track. How does it feel? How is it different to dance to? Why do you think this might be? Is it slower/faster, punchier/smoother? Having the dancers choose their own music can really engage them, particularly ones who think that maypole is uncool or irrelevant to them and their culture.

Folk music rhythms

In the dance descriptions we have used terms like *Jigs*, *Reels*, *Polkas* and *Hornpipes* to describe the tunes. Don't panic: listen to the CD and you will get the idea! However, here is a quick guide:

Jigs	6/8 time, great for skipping e.g. *Humpty Dumpty*
Polkas	2/4 with a lift at the end of each bar e.g. *Little Brown Jug*
Marches	2/4 like polkas, but with a more even feel e.g. *The Grand old Duke of York*
Reels	4/4 and much smoother so that they roll along like *The Blue Peter Theme*
Hornpipes	4/4 time, usually dotted rhythms, great for step-hopping e.g. *Waltzing Matilda*

Can you follow the music you are dancing to?

The good news is that, no matter how complicated the tune may sound, most English dance music has a clear structure. Since the 18th century, this has meant phrases of 4 or 8 bars which then build up the whole tune. The most common version of this is an 8 bar 'A' part, played twice, followed by an 8-bar 'B' part, played twice, known in the trade as an 'A-A-B-B' tune.

Here are some fun activities to try:

Activity 1

Sit and listen, asking dancers to punch the air at the start of a phrase. How many counts can they find in a phrase?* Split the group into two halves, one to dance/move around the space on the first phrase, the other to move on the second phrase and so on.

Activity 2

Combine Activity 1 with the Homing Pigeons warm-up *(p18)*. The aim is for dancers to get back into place at the end of a phrase - not before, not after!

Activity 3

Create a series of 4 actions, e.g. marching, skipping, arm jive, stepping from side to side. Do each one for 8 bars, then change. Can the dancers manage to change at the right time without following your lead? Can they count silently through a section of music and come in with the next part of the sequence at the start of the next phrase of music?

N.B. Being able to count the beats and/or bars is a useful skill, but an instinctive awareness of the phrases is even more helpful in the long run. It's surprising how readily people start to tune into the start and end points of phrases, even though you might need to count at the outset.

Getting started

Preparation for each dance

With all the ribbon dances, preparation is key. We cannot stress enough how important it is to make sure that everyone is standing in the right place with the ribbon held correctly, and that they know what they should be doing. Almost all the dances are made up of quite simple actions so if the preparation is done well then the dances are much more likely to go smoothly. It is easier to spend a bit more time getting ready than trying to correct things as everyone is moving – believe us, we have tried! With this in mind, you will see that every dance has a *'Before You Begin'* section, which we would encourage you to take note of before moving into *'Making the Pattern'*.

Holding the ribbons

Lifting the ribbon with tensioning hand

There are a number of possible variations. We favour holding the loop in one hand, getting a good grip as though walking the dog, and using the other hand further up the ribbon to maintain control and tension. Ideally the ribbon should be kept straight at all times but not so taut as to move the pole. This keeps a better visual image than if the ribbons are allowed to sag, and the patterns form more easily and neatly. Where possible, the hand in the loop should be that which is further away from the pole, i.e. the right hand when moving anti-clockwise.

Although it is usually best to keep two hands on the ribbon, it is sometimes necessary to use only one hand – this is fine, but don't let

go! Be sure not to let your dancers wrap the ribbon around their wrist as this can be dangerous.

More dancers than ribbons?

In any session there are likely to be more dancers than ribbons. Ask for the relevant number of volunteers to miss the first dance and then, when repeating the dance or moving onto another one, get them to approach one of the dancers, tap them on the shoulder and ask "please may I have your ribbon?" The ribbon then passes from one to another without being allowed to fall to the ground. The next time, you can ask those dancers who have already done both dances to hold their ribbons up high and so on. This usually works well and allows everyone to get an even amount of dancing. Emphasise the importance of watching the dance and ask questions of those not dancing before unwinding any pattern. Those on the outside do have a different view and they can actively help in improving the dances.

Much of this also applies in performance, although it is usually preferable to have each dancer knowing which ribbon they are taking and so on.

Check out *Inclusion* (p12-14) for more ways to keep waiting dancers actively engaged.

Taking up the ribbons

The ribbons need to be in the correct order, and handing them out is helpful. Here are some options:

For teaching:

• One person hands out all of the ribbons, doing this four at a time;

• Two people start from the same point in the circle and work in opposite directions.

For shows:

• To prevent the wind tangling the ribbons, keep them secured until needed;

• Send out a team to take four or eight ribbons each to hand out when dancers are in position.

Ribbon colours

In general, we teach the dances by referring to ribbon colours: the dancers do not need to remember 'inners' or 'outers', 'odds' or 'evens' etc.. This keeps things simple and everyone

has a visual reminder of 'who they are' in their hands.

To make this work, arrange the ribbons so that two colours alternate on the outer ring of the crown and two on the inner. We have used this convention in the instructions with the Red & Blue ribbons on the Outer Ring, and Yellow and Green on the Inner. Of course, this is purely arbitrary and you might want to vary it to suit the ribbons you have, school colours etc.. Great - it's part of creating your own tradition.

Choosing your dance

As with any form of teaching, it is best to start simply and work up. The first five dances are a proven sequence that leads to the ever popular 'Plait'. After that, there are additional simple dances for younger or less experienced groups which give variety and fun without added complexity. And then there are some which will challenge even the most experienced dancer. Each dance has an approximate rating (1 = easy, 4 = difficult), but no-one knows your dancers better than you. Choose accordingly!

Dance creation

Any of these dances can be used as dances in their own right. However, you can also think of them as components or 'figures' which can be used to make any number of variations or combinations...

Dance activity

Each colour in turn dances 8 steps into the middle and back out to place. Repeat with 2 colours at a time, finishing with all 4 colours simultaneously. More proficient dancers can experiment with tensioning their ribbons for greater effect.

Making a show

Dancing on

When it comes to a performance, you will need to decide how to get the dancers into position and ready to dance. Here are a few options to try, which may be done with or without music:

Single file

Line up your 24 dancers in order: red, green, blue, yellow, red, green, blue, yellow, etc. Dance on into starting places, making sure that the dancers lead round in the correct direction to keep the same order and orientation of colours around the pole.

Promenade hold

Line up your 24 dancers in pairs: red with green, blue with yellow, red with green, blue with yellow, etc.. Dance on and into place using a promenade hold, face in, and let go of hands. It doesn't matter whether this dance is done clockwise or anticlockwise - the important thing is for the same colour to be on the same side of each pair, and for them to face in as a couple so the order remains the same. The dancers should now be alternately red, green, blue, yellow around the circle.

Finishing the dance

Dance over... Job done? Nearly, but the ending and exit from a dance leave a lasting impression. Here are some things to think about:

Releasing the ribbons

The simplest and most fun way to end a dance is to hold the ribbon between the thumb and index finger, gently pull back on the ribbons, and release them with a 'ping'. Children enjoy preceding this with 'wiggly worms', gently shaking their ribbon to make pretty waves up towards the pole. They may, of course, have other ideas as to how to finish with a flourish....!

Dancing off

The simplest way to dance off is to circle in single file, with one child being designated to lead the line out. Again, the dancers may have their own ideas about how to finish with more of a bang!

Key points

Make sure your dancers line up in the right order to match their dance positions, and that they lead on in the right direction! You may laugh, but you don't want it to go wrong before the dance has even started!

If several groups are performing at the same event, do they all need the same number and configuration of ribbons? If not, you will need to build time into the performance to lower the crown and rearrange the ribbons.

How much space?

A standard Maypole (Educational Aids or similar) requires a dance space 7m in diameter, and 3.5m in height. If you are short of space, there are some other possibilities - give us a call and we will be happy to advise.

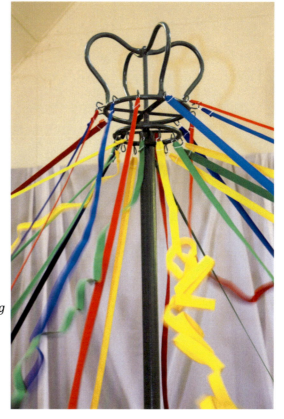

Releasing the ribbons with a 'ping'

Period and performance costumes

Wearing any sort of costume can really enhance any performance. Looking at those earliest pictures it is unlikely that people did then as it was clearly a community event, but later theatrical shows would definitely have had costumes. Later on, the Victorians would either have had lovely floaty costumes for the girls and breeches for the boys, or something pretending to be Tudor or Medieval.

Since the dances we have given you include Tudor, Victorian and Modern, the choice of costume is yours. Sports kit or school uniform is perfectly valid. You might try using coloured shirts or, for girls, simple skirts in bright colours. Another option is to make simple tabards or tatter jackets.

The most important thing is to make sure that, whatever you wear, it is not going to hamper the dancing. For instance, skirts that can be trodden on or very tall hats could obviously cause problems. It can be a good idea for dancers to practise in their costumes before the performance, just to make sure that they can be moved in freely.

All dances in this book are described

with the ribbons as follows:

Outer ring:

RED & BLUE

Inner Ring:

GREEN & YELLOW

CIRCLING

LEVEL: 1   SUGGESTED TRACKS: 1 or 9 (Jigs or Reels)

SUMMARY: Possibly the simplest dance there is: just dancing in a circle around the pole while holding the ribbons.

While this is a very simple dance it does create a pattern with a fixed crown Maypole. With an Educational Aids style maypole it actually creates two patterns and teaches beginners to all move together.

DANCE INSTRUCTIONS

Before you Begin:

- Give out the ribbons. Make sure that all dancers are holding the loop in the right hand, with the left hand controlling the tension. With this hold, it will be natural for all dancers to turn to the right, or anti-clockwise.

- Are the dancers making a good, even circle, keeping the ribbons taut but not pulling on the pole?

Making the Pattern:

1. All turn to the right and dance anti-clockwise around the pole;

2. As the dance progresses, the ribbons on the inner ring will wrap around the pole while those on the outer ring remain free.

Fig 1: Circling anti-clockwise, with the ribbon held in the outside hand

The Unwind:

1. Stop and use the break in the music to change hands holding the ribbon;

2. All turn to the left and dance back to place.

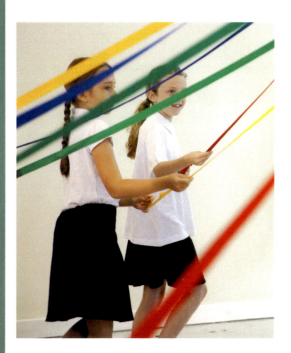

Dance at a Glance

1. Circle right;

2. Stop and turn round;

3. Circle left.

Extra Activity: Dancing in a Circle

Without holding ribbons, ask your dancers to face in towards the pole, standing at arms' length to the person next to them. Now all turn to the right and walk or skip around in a circle. What happens to the circle? More often than not, the circle will become uneven and get smaller and smaller.

Try again, making sure that everyone starts at arms' length again. This time look across at the person opposite them, and try to stay opposite them as the circle moves. What happened to the circle this time? Was it even? Did it change size or shape?

Now try once more, but this time following the **outside** shoulder of the person in front, trying to stay the same distance away from them all the time.

Ideally, the best way to maintain your circle is to keep half an eye on the person opposite, whilst trying to follow the outside shoulder of the person in front. Keep practising!

Performance Tips:

*   Make sure that dancers are holding the ribbon correctly: good ribbon technique now will save you time later on;

*   Are the dancers evenly spaced? Are they holding the ribbons with good control and tension?

BARBER'S POLE

LEVEL: 2   SUGGESTED TRACKS: 3 or 9 (Jigs)

SUMMARY: A development of Circling with the inner and outer circles moving in opposite directions. Creates two separate spirals around the pole.

A very traditional dance that appears wherever there are Maypoles. John Ruskin gave it this name because, with Red & White ribbons, it resembles a Barbers Pole, the colours originally signifying blood and flesh which were the main components of the barber surgeon's trade.

DANCE INSTRUCTIONS

Before you Begin:

Make sure that:

- The Reds and Blues know who is on either side of them - they will all need to return to this place at the end of the dance.

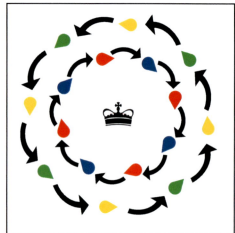

- Those holding the ribbons that are attached to the outer ring (Red & Blue) need to take a step or two in towards the pole and turn to the right. Those on the Inner Ring (Green and Yellow) remain on the outside and turn to the left.

- The dancers are holding the ribbons correctly and that those now on the outside (Yellow & Green) know how to use their controlling (inner) hand to lift the ribbons clear of oncoming dancers. It is sometimes and idea to swap very small or young dancers into the middle.

Stepping for Maypole Dances

While learning the dance we almost always insist that it is walked initially. Concentrating on the ribbons to start with is essential. Once the dance is mastered, then is the time to introduce some sort of stepping, usually skipping, but make sure everyone actually knows what the step is. More technically advanced dancers may also try to face in towards the centre and travel using a sideways *slip step* or *gallop,* which can give the dance a more dramatic feel.

Making the Pattern:

1. All circle in the direction you are facing. Initially just get one group of dancers to dance in the direction they are facing for two phrases of music. Then repeat with the other group;

2. Remind those now on the inside (Greens & Yellows) that they may need to duck!

This picture shows what you need to do, but with the greens and yellows on the inside.

Dance at a Glance

All face into the centre.

1. Reds & Blues take 2 steps in and turn right.

2. Yellows & Greens turn to the left.

EITHER

3a. Inners dance then stop;

3b. Outers dance then stop;

3c. Repeat steps 1 and 2 as desired;

OR

3. All dance in the direction you are facing

---

4. *Pause to change direction and unwind.*

The Unwind:

1. Stop and turn around to face in the opposite direction around the pole. Change hand hold so that the loop is held in the outside hand;

2. Dance until the pattern is unwound and dancers are nearly back where they began. Stop the music and dancers, and ask them to look for the people they started the dance with, so that they can rejoin the outer circle in their original places.

Performance Tips:

- Practise skipping neatly and in time with the music.

- Listen to the phrasing so that this becomes more instinctive than counted. You might like to try the exercises in the *Music* section *(p21).*

Next Steps:

- There is a variation of this dance where the dancers, once they have completed a full circle, change places with the person they started the dance next to, so that the outers now become the inners and vice versa.

- Can you find a Barber's Pole outside a shop near you?

- See Challenges *(p51).*

CHRYSANTHEMUM

LEVEL: 1 SUGGESTED TRACKS: 2 or 6 (Polkas)

SUMMARY: A very simple dance with only 1/4 of the dancers moving at any one time. Works particularly well for a disparity of ages, uneven numbers, and differently abled dancers.

This is a very simple dance originally created by Chris Turner and described in *Dancing Round the Maypole*. We have adapted to make it even simpler to teach.

In this dance, one colour goes into the middle, turns to the left, and makes a single, clockwise circuit of the pole before returning home. This is repeated by each colour in turn. With a little imagination, the pattern resembles the long petals of a chrysanthemum...

The turn of the Reds! Look at the even spacing.

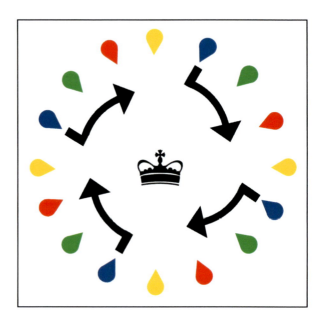

Dance at a Glance

1. Blues* move in and circle the pole once, clockwise;

2. Repeat with Reds, Greens & Yellows;

3. Continue sequence as desired;

4. Yellows start the unwind.

Colour sequence arbitrary

Stepping

This can be a walk, a skip or something more complicated suggested by whatever music you choose. However if you continue the dance for more than a few turns each, then stepping will become much harder. Much better to concentrate on the phrasing for this one.

DANCE INSTRUCTIONS

Before you Begin:

Make sure that:

- Everyone knows what colour ribbon they are holding!

- Your dancers know their position in the circle. Who is on either side of them?

Making the Pattern:

1. All face into the middle, holding the ribbon with the right hand raised;

2. All the **Blues*** take 2 steps towards the pole and turn to the left. When everyone is ready, dance once around the pole and back to place;

3. Stand facing into the middle again with the right hand raised;

4. **Repeat steps 1, 2 and 3 with the Reds, Greens and Yellows*.** This can be repeated as often as the enthusiasm and concentration of the dancers allows, usually two or three times. For really young dancers, once might be enough!

*The choice and sequence of colours is completely arbitrary, but be consistent once you have started.

The Unwind:

Starting with the last colour to have moved (in this case Yellow), reverse the sequence and direction of dance until the pattern is completely unwound.

It's getting harder now the pattern is lower—duck!

Performance Tips:

- Each colour becomes a team, helping each other know when to start, and moving at the same speed - it's not a race to the finish!

- Listen to phrasing so that this becomes more instinctive than counted *(see p18)*.

Next Steps:

- Add an introduction or coda by getting the dancers to go in and out, either all together, or by colour group.

- Add extra flourishes by turning underneath your own ribbon, or parading around the pole.

- See Challenges *(p51)*.

COBWEB

SUMMARY: All ribbons of the same colour dance in turn around the next person creating a Cobweb pattern. Great for introducing stepping and rhythm.

Developed by Mike from a dance called *The Accumulator* written by Chris Turner. Cobweb is great for helping the dancers to handle the ribbons, leaving them freer to think about steps and phrasing. The pattern is what it says on the tin!

Not to be confused with Spider's Web, this dance involves everyone and is easier to teach.

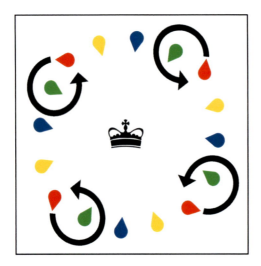

Fig. 1: *The moving dancer passes behind and over the ribbon to the right*

Dance at a Glance

Arrange ribbons in order e.g. Yellow, Blue, Red, Green. All dancers take a step in towards the pole.

1. **Reds** around **Greens**
   (over to the right and back to place);

2. Repeat with Greens, Yellows & Blues in turn;

3. Repeat sequence as many times as ribbons allow;

4. Unwind with EITHER Yellows going around Reds (under to the right) OR Reds going around Yellows (over to the left).

Fig. 2: *The moving dancer ducks under and back to place*

DANCE INSTRUCTIONS

Before you Begin:

- Make sure that all the ribbons are in the same order around the pole, e.g. Red, Green, Blue, Yellow going in an anti-clockwise direction.

Making the Pattern:

1. All take a small step in so it is possible for dancers to travel around the outside;

2. With left hand raised, all ribbons should be held reasonably high, around head height if possible. All face in towards the pole;

3. The **Reds** turn to their **right** and dance around the **Greens**, going over and behind first *(Fig. 1)*, then coming back underneath to their places *(Fig. 2)*;

4. **Greens** repeat this movement, dancing around the **Blues** and back to place;

5. **Blues** then dance around **Yellows**, followed by **Yellows** around the **Reds**;

6. Everyone take a small step in towards the pole and tighten the ribbons before repeating. The length of the ribbons is usually the limiting factor.

The Unwind:

To undo the pattern you can, as usual, just completely reverse the process OR:

Instead, have the **Reds** going to their **left** around the **Yellows** by going **over** first again – try it! We think this looks better as lifting the ribbons at the start of each figure is visually better than ducking underneath.

The finished pattern

Performance Tips:

- It helps if the ribbons are held firmly and, when the dancers are going underneath, to dance further in towards the centre.

- Older dancers enjoy performing this dance to a hornpipe or 'step-hop' to give a stronger rhythmic drive to the movements. Try Track 8 on the CD.

- As ¾ of the dancers are standing still, it is fun for them to create a chant for the dance e.g. *'The cat's got the measles, the measles, the measles...'* etc.

Standing Still With Purpose!

- Encourage the static dancers to feel part of the performance, not only waiting to dance, but providing tension to form the pattern evenly. Standing still "helpfully", i.e. ducking or lifting ribbons is crucial.

SINGLE PLAIT

LEVEL: 3   SUGGESTED TRACKS: 2 or 3 (Steady Jigs)

SUMMARY: Closed plait around the pole created by the dancers weaving around the circle.

This classic Maypole dance appears in traditions from around the world and in lots of historical illustrations. It's a dance that everyone wants to do, but timing can often be an issue for beginners. Here we give a version of the dance, devised by Mike, which makes sure that it will work first time for almost everyone. Then, when you are ready, you can move on to the more traditional way of dancing it.

DANCE INSTRUCTIONS

Before you Begin:

- All the **Reds** and **Blues** turn to the right to face anti-clockwise around the pole.

- All the **Yellows** and **Greens** turn to the left to face clockwise around the pole.

- At this point it is worth checking that everyone has done this successfully, is facing someone and has the loop held in the hand furthest from the pole.

Fig. 1: 'Reds & Blues over'

Fig. 2: 'Yellows & Greens over'

Dance at a Glance

Order ribbons: Red, Green, Blue, Yellow. Reds & Blues face right, Yellows & Greens face left.

VERSION 1:

1. 'Reds & Blues over';

2. 'Yellows & Greens over';

3. Continue to call alternate colours.

VERSION 2:

1. 'Reds & Blues weave';

2. 'Yellows & Greens weave';

3. Repeat 1 & 2 if required.

VERSION 3:

1. All weave (Reds & Blues over first).

ALL: Stop & unwind

Making the Pattern:

Here are 3 ways to make the pattern. The first assumes no previous experience:

Arts students seeing how far they can go… (University of London, Arts), May 1st 2013

Version 1

1. **Reds** and **Blues** go over one person (Yellows and Greens stand still but duck if necessary);

2. **Yellows** and **Greens** go over one person (Reds and Blues stand still);

3. Repeat this pattern for as long as you want.

Version 2

1. **Reds** and **Blues** weave over and under the others until back home (moving anti-clockwise);

2. Repeat with **Yellows** and **Greens** dancing clockwise once around and back to place.

When the dancers are confident with this, try…

Version 3

In this version, everyone moves at the same time.

1. **Reds** and **Blues** go over WHILE Yellows & Greens go under;

2. **Yellows** and **Greens** go over one person WHILE Reds and Blues go under;

3. Continue weaving in this way.

Fig.3: Green goes over

The Unwind:

To unwind the pattern, repeat the dance in reverse. Make sure that everyone is facing the correct way around the pole before you begin.

Performance Tips:

- Always keep an eye on the top of your ribbon. If a mistake has been made on the way, it will need to be undone in reverse to be fixed. Put another way, if you make a mistake on the way there, it won't be solved by dancing the figure 'correctly' on the unwind.

- **Sinuous or Mechanical?** When dancers have become confident with the traditional style of this dance (Version 3), the pattern of weaving is a series of curves or waves. An alternative was discovered by a group dancing to a really powerful piece of music with a strong rock beat. To make sure that they all moved together, they brought the ribbons up or down sharply at the beginning of every other bar (i.e. Up & 2 & 3 & 4; Down & 2 & 3 & 4…) which worked incredibly well and gave such a strong mechanical feel, it almost became a new dance. Try it and see what you think!

DOUBLE PLAIT

LEVEL: 3   SUGGESTED TRACKS: 2 (Steady Jigs) **or 7** (Jigs)

SUMMARY: The same dance as Single Plait but with dancers working in pairs. Useful for mixed ability groups including dancers who want a challenge.

Dancing in pairs offers new options for The Plait:

- Increases the space for dancing (see below)
- Doubles the number of dancers by having 2 dancers per ribbon (not shown)
- Lets stronger dancers help those less confident
- Makes a major change to how the dance looks and how it works

DANCE INSTRUCTIONS

Before you Begin:
- Pair up Reds with Greens to face anti-clockwise, and Blues with Yellows to face clockwise. Dancers should stand next to their 'partner', facing the same way.

Holding the Ribbons:
- Our preferred way of holding the ribbons (and there are many) is for the dancer on the outside to hold both loops in the outside hand and place their other hand further up the ribbon for control. The person on the inside then places their hands alternately on the ribbon creating a sort of crossed hand hold like a promenade in country dancing.

Dance at a Glance

Arrange the dancers in pairs (Red with Green; Yellow with Blue):

1. Pairs face (Red & Green anti-clockwise; Yellow & Blue clockwise);

2. Weave, with Red & Green passing **under** first;

3. Stop and unwind.

Reds and Greens duck under

Making the Pattern:

The dance is then very similar to the Single Plait.

1. **Reds** and **Greens** go under while Yellows and Blues keep dancing forwards, lifting the ribbons;*

2. **Yellows** and **Blues** go under while Reds and Greens keep dancing forwards, lifting the ribbons.

*The dancers need to be aware of the circle that they start in and not step outside it because this can cause the pole to tilt. Hence the dancers need to think about going UNDER each time rather than over as for the Single Plait.

The Unwind:

To unwind the plait, turn around and retrace your steps. Keep an eye on the ribbons as any mistakes made on the way there will need to be corrected on the way back!

Double Plait, Chelsea

Performance Tips:

Do your dancers work well in pairs? Without ribbons, practise a promenade hold *(p6)* and have alternate couples weave their way around the circle and back to place.

- Are the pairs aware of the other dancers? Can all the pairs work together, moving in and out at the same time with the music?

3 in Hand:

If you have access to a larger pole or longer ribbons, you might like to try 3 dancers per ribbon, or 3 dancers with their ribbons held together. Should you want to include it then it should not be too difficult for dancers to work out how, based on what they have learnt up to now. As with the Double Plait, the most complicated part is working out a ribbon and hand hold that works for each group of dancers.

SPIDER'S WEB

LEVEL: 3   SUGGESTED TRACKS: 8 or 5

SUMMARY: This dance is a little harder and uses half the dancers to create an open plait web pattern by dancing around the other dancers who are acting as posts.

The Spiders Web is one of the most traditional of dances and because of its name and distinctive pattern tends to stay in the memory. However it takes plenty of practice to get the timing right for a good display, especially when danced to the traditional tune *All Things Bright & Beautiful* (or *The 29th of May*).

DANCE INSTRUCTIONS

Before you Begin:

- All the dancers on the Outer Ring (Yellows & Greens) take a step towards the pole and stand still, keeping their ribbons taut and being prepared to duck or move slightly as the other dancers go past. Visually it is best for these 'posts' to turn and face out, holding the ribbon over their right shoulder *(Fig. 1)*.

Dance at a Glance

Arrange the dancers in pairs (Red with Green; Yellow with Blue):

1. Greens & Yellows step in;

2. Reds & Blues dance around the person to their right;

3. Reds & Blues move onto the next;

4. Repeat steps 2 & 3 until the ribbons are too short to continue;

5. Stop & unwind;

6. Greens & Yellows return to place in the outer circle.

Fig. 1: The post faces out with the ribbon on his right shoulder

Making the Pattern:

Assuming that Yellows and Greens are static, Reds and Blues are the travelling dancers. Reds and Blues turn to their right and:

1. Dance around the person to the right, going outside them then underneath and inside back to place;

2. Go behind the same person once more to move on one place;

3. Now dance around the next person and back to this new place;

4. Move on and repeat this figure as long as the ribbons allow. If the 'posts' move in a little more, then it can be possible to keep the dance going for longer.

The Unwind:

1. To unwind the dance, Blues and Reds need to retrace their steps until they are back home;

2. Greens and Yellows return to their place in the outer circle.

If you want all dancers to have a turn at dancing the pattern, the dance can be repeated with Reds & Blues acting as posts, and Greens and Yellows travelling.

Performance Tips:

*   Encourage the static dancers to stand tall and proud with good ribbon tension to maintain the pattern. Their role is really important! If you want all your dancers to have an equal chance to move, repeat with the other half dancing. Can you make the changeover flow?

*   What can the 'posts' observe about the dance from their position? Can they make any suggestions to improve the performance? If you plan to swap roles after the first dance, can they be thinking about what they will need to do when it is their turn to move?

Next Steps:

*   Another variation is to have the posts move in further towards the pole and kneel down, still facing out with the ribbon over the right shoulder. Make sure that there is room for the moving dancers to pass behind them without tripping over feet or ribbons. This variation is a simple way to add visual interest to your performance and enable the pattern to be danced for longer.

*   Try the dance with different types of music, something with a different feel might make it work even better for you.

*   Compare this dance with *Cobweb (p32)*. Which do you prefer? Why?

ROPES

LEVEL: 1   SUGGESTED TRACKS: 7 or 9 (Jigs)

SUMMARY: One of two dances that create a simple pattern of plaits radiating out from the pole. Great fun and especially good for people with excess energy to spare!

Because of its simplicity this has not always been included in collections but it can be really helpful in teaching basic techniques to younger dancers or as part of a display.

DANCE INSTRUCTIONS

Before you Begin:

- Make sure that all the dancers are holding their ribbons correctly and facing the centre with no ribbons crossed. Pair the dancers (Red with Green; Blue with Yellow).

Making the Pattern:

- Reds and Blues stand still, facing the centre. Yellows and Greens simply dance anti-clockwise around the person to their right, their 'partner', as many times as they can so that the two ribbons are wrapped together. Keep dancing until the cue to stop, or the ribbons are too short to continue.

Yellow dances around his partner

The Unwind:

- To unwind, it is now the turn of Reds and Blues to dance. Reds and Blues stand still facing the pole, and their partners (Yellow and Green) dance clockwise around them until all the twists are undone.

Dance at a Glance

1. Reds & Blues stand still, facing the pole;

2. Yellows & Greens dance anti-clockwise around and around the dancer to their right ('partner');

3. To unwind, Yellows & Greens stand still. Reds & Blues dance clockwise around their partner.

Keep dancing as long as the ribbons allow

SILKSTREAM

LEVEL: 2   SUGGESTED TRACKS: 4 & 5 (Reels / Jigs)

SUMMARY: A sequel to Ropes. The same dance but with everyone moving at once with an added display feature.

Silkstream was devised by Mike when his planned, more complex, dance went very wrong! Its rather chaotic appearance, energy and competitive element were an immediate success. Great for any lively group of dancers and a vivid contrast to some of the more complex technical dances.

DANCE INSTRUCTIONS

Before you Begin:

- Pair the dancers as for Ropes (Red with Green, Blue with Yellow).

Making the Pattern:

1. Just ask them to dance around each other, moving at the same time as quickly as possible to fast music *(e.g. Track 4)*! Instant chaos and enjoyment generally ensue, with some dancers managing to work out the most efficient way of doing this by controlling the ribbons;

2. Once the paired ribbons have been twisted far enough, stop the music and the dancers;

3. Change the music to something steadier *(e.g. Track 5)*;

4. All dancers turn to their left and parade ONCE around the pole in a clockwise direction, stopping when they get back home. This creates a slightly different pattern at the top of the pole and gives a useful period of calm in the dance.

Dance at a Glance

Pair dancers: Red with Green; Blue with Yellow.

1. FAST MUSIC: Pairs dance around each other as fast as possible and as many times as they can;

2. STEADY MUSIC: All parade once around the pole and back;

3. FAST MUSIC: Pairs unwind the twists and sit down when finished, still holding the ribbons.

The Unwind:

1. All face anti-clockwise and parade back to their starting places;

2. Once home, change the music to the faster track, and unravel by dancing around each other again;

3. Tell the dancers to sit down as soon as they have finished, **keeping hold of the ribbons**. This makes it easier for those still unwinding, and adds a competitive element for those who like a race!

HELTER SKELTER

LEVEL: 4   SUGGESTED TRACKS: 14

SUMMARY: Dancers work one at a time to create an asymmetrical plait from the pole. A truly unique dance.

This dance was devised for a circle dance group. They had elected a May Queen for the day and wanted a solo dance for her. This inevitably removed any ideas of symmetry. Once the pattern had started, we realised that everyone could have a go, and the pattern of an open plait spiralling away from the pole was the result.

This figure came from a Tudor dance called the *Brawle da Montarde*, one that is often danced nowadays as the *Horse's Brawle*.

DANCE INSTRUCTIONS

Before you Begin:

- All dancers face the pole holding the ribbons taut;

- All take a good step in so that other dancers can pass behind them;

- Identify a lead dancer, *Dancer 1*;

- Identify *Dancer 2* (the dancer to the right of *Dancer 1*), *Dancer 3* and so on.

All face in towards the pole

Dance at a Glance

1. All step in;

2. Dancer 1 weaves to right (over first);

3. Dancer 2 follows and so on;

4. Unwind in reverse.

Making the Pattern:

1. Dancer 1 turns to the right and starts to weave around the circle, going over Dancer 2, under Dancer 3 and so on. The static dancers should 'stand still helpfully,' lifting their ribbons, ducking or moving in as necessary;

2. Dancer 1 continues to weave all the way back to place;

3. Meanwhile, when Dancer 1 has travelled about four or five places around the circle, Dancer 2 begins to weave, following the direction of Dancer 1 and going over first;

4. Dancer 3 begins likewise. Eventually everyone will have a turn at dancing one complete circuit of the pole until the pattern is finished.

Dancer 1 weaves under and over while the others stand still 'helpfully'

Keep plaiting until everyone has had a turn

The Unwind:

We have not discovered any option for unwinding this dance except to do the whole sequence in reverse. This does take a lot of concentration, particularly for the static dancers, who can be very helpful to those dancing past them by keeping an eye on the pattern and spotting any errors as they happen.

Performance Tips:

- Take your time!! If one dancer gets a bit confused, don't crowd them—it will just make it harder! Keep your distance while they think. Above all, remember the golden rule of Maypole Dancing: NO OVERTAKING!!!

Next Steps:

- Think about the stepping used, and how this can be used to improve the making of the pattern. Can you find a stepping pattern that enables all the travelling dancers to move inwards and outwards at the same time?

TWISTER

LEVEL: 3   SUGGESTED TRACKS: 3 or 7 (Jigs or Reels)

SUMMARY: Dancers in turn change places with the dancer opposite them on the other side of the pole, creating two spiral plaits. Fun to dance and visually stunning.

This dance is the result of a student at a teacher training session saying "what if..?" We tried and this dance happened! There are many more dances out there to be discovered, often as simple as this. The unwind came from a group of Year 9 performing arts students at Bowland Academy.

DANCE INSTRUCTIONS

Before you Begin:

- Each dancer needs to identify the person opposite them in circle, their 'partner' for this dance. If you have 24 dancers, this should be someone with the same colour ribbon.

- Choose one pair to start the dance.

Fig 1: A blue pair swap places, passing to the left of the pole

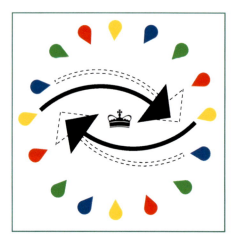

Making the Pattern:

1. The first couple change places with each other, passing to the left of the pole i.e. moving clockwise. It can help to think of the pole as being a mini-roundabout or traffic bollard: dancers must always pass to the left of the pole, no matter where they start from *(Fig. 1)*;

2. This movement is repeated by the next couple to their left;

3. Keep repeating this sequence as many times as you want. If dancers are alert, there is no need to wait for the previous couple to return to place before the next one begins. In fact, if dancers become really proficient, it is possible to have up to three couples moving at once. The trick here is to catch the eye of your partner before starting to move.

Fig 2: As the group circles, the plait begins to split into 2 parts from the pole

The Unwind:

It is possible to unwind Twister by simply dancing the action in reverse, keeping to the right of the pole i.e. anti-clockwise and concentrating hard. However, there is a different and, to our minds, more elegant option.

1. All dancers turn to the right and travel anti-clockwise around the pole in single file. Continue to unwind in this way until, eventually, there are two plaits radiating outwards on opposite sides of the pole *(Fig. 2)*;

2. At this point, the dancers separate into two groups, **working independently to unwind each plait**. Each group forms their own oval shape, dancing clockwise **without going around the pole** *(Fig. 3)*. Make sure the ribbons are held high at this point to avoid dancing on the base of the pole. It can help to have a helper standing near the base of the pole to help establish the pathway of each group *(Fig. 4)*.

Fig 3: Each group works separately, dancing in an oval to unwind their plait

Fig 4: A traffic warden can direct dancers and prevent collisions with the pole!

Dance at a Glance

1. First pair change places (keeping to the left of the pole);

2. Second pair (to their left), repeat, and so on;

3. To unwind, all parade anti-clockwise until the plaits are free from the pole;

4. Separate into two separate groups, with both plaits dancing anti-clockwise until fully unwound.

Performance Tips:

- Once dancers understand the pattern, they can begin to work on achieving even spacing within each oval. How fast does each oval travel? Can they adjust their speeds to finish the unwind at the same time?

EASTER PLAIT

LEVEL: 3   SUGGESTED TRACKS: 1 or 7 (Jigs/Reels)

SUMMARY: A slightly more challenging dance creating 3-ribbon plaits radiating out from the pole. Good for small team working.

Mike first used this dance at an event in the village of High Easter in Essex. They had done the main dances around their big outdoor pole when the weather turned, moving them inside. Twelve girls wanted to carry on dancing, and this was the result. For them it was like plaiting hair. For folk dancers it is a figure called a hey or a reel with added ribbons.

DANCE INSTRUCTIONS

Before you Begin:

- Start by arranging the dancers into groups of three around the pole. These dancers work exclusively together.

- All face in towards the pole.

Dance at a Glance

1. Arrange the dancers into groups of 3 around the pole;

2. Plait the ribbons by the outsides changing alternately into the middle of the group;

3. Undo in reverse.

Making the Pattern:

Each plait is made by the outside dancers alternately changing into the middle of the group. The sequence is exactly like plaiting hair, which may be more helpful to some dancers than others!

1. The dancer on the right swaps places with the middle dancer by passing over and on the outside;

2. The dancer on the left swaps places with the dancer who is now in the middle, again passing over and on the outside;

3. This pattern continues, right then left, right then left and so on.

Dancers work in groups of 3 to weave their plaits

Dance pattern

When the movement starts to flow, the dancers may realise that they are all travelling in a figure of eight pattern. This is called a hey or reel in country dancing and is a very useful figure to learn. Of course, if the dancers have already learnt this in country dancing, the above teaching may be unnecessary!

The Unwind:

Having made the plaits, you can choose whether or not to parade with them. After this, the plaits are simply unwound by dancing the action in reverse. In rehearsal, you might want to introduce a competitive element, as with Silkstream, seeing which group can be the first to finish and sit down!

Performance Tips:

- Try to make the dance flow within each group of 3.

- Listen to the music and experiment with ways to make the movements fit the phrasing.

- Can all the groups of 3 work at the same rate to make the plaits? Are the plaits even?

Next Steps:

- See *Challenges (p51).*

JACOB'S LADDER

LEVEL: 4   **SUGGESTED TRACKS: 6** (Steady)

SUMMARY: This dance is a real challenge but if your dancers are already good at working in small groups see what they can make of it. Working in groups of four they create a ladder or lattice effect radiating out from the pole.

Mike found this dance in an old book by Sandy Mason and it had apparently been created by children during a series of workshops at Sidmouth International Festival. They were probably all quite experienced dancers already. This is certainly different and requires really good technique with the ribbons to make the pattern work.

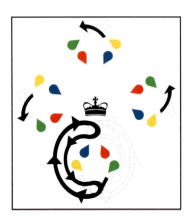

DANCE INSTRUCTIONS

Before you Begin:

- The outer ribbons (Reds and Blues), take two steps forward and hold their ribbons taut. They now do nothing except stand still 'helpfully'. In the learning stages, these two dancers can play an important role in helping to direct operations!

Fig. 1: Standing still helpfully! The ribbons need to be further apart to maintain the lattice.

Dance at a Glance

Reds & Blues step forward and hold ribbons taut.

Yellows & Greens:

1. Move behind Reds & Blues and turn to face;

2. Loop around each other, passing right shoulders;

3. Dance around Reds & Blues to meet inside;

4. Loop around each other;

5. Dance around Reds & Blues to meet outside;

Repeat while ribbon allows, then unwind.

Making the Pattern:

The dancing couple (Yellows and Greens):

Fig. 2: Green and yellow are standing behind the posts. They are about to loop around each other before retracing their steps

1. Move so they are directly behind the 'posts' (Reds & Blues) and turn to face each other *(Fig. 2)*;

2. Loop around each other, passing right shoulders, finishing back in place but facing away from each other;

3. Dance forwards in the way they are facing and around the posts to meet on the inside, quite close to the pole;

4. In these positions, loop around each other once more, ending facing away from each other again;

Fig. 3: Green and yellow repeat the movement, this time in front of the posts

5. Dance forwards in the way they are facing and around the posts to meet on the outside. Repeat this pattern until the rungs of a ladder have been woven all the way down the static ribbons.

N.B. The dancing couple always pass by the same post on the same side.

The Unwind:

Celebrate a successful pattern, then unwind by dancing the above in reverse!

Performance Tips:

- The skill here is that the Reds and Blues need to keep the ribbons taut while the Yellows and Greens need to keep them quite loose. If they make the first loop around the Reds and Blues fairly big, they can 'lay' the first strut of the pattern, or 'rung of the ladder,' high up the supports.

- Just getting the pattern to work is enough of a challenge for most people. The next step is to phrase it so that it fits the music.

WATER WHEEL

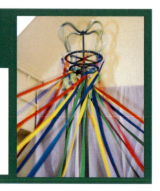

LEVEL: 1   SUGGESTED TRACKS: 5 (Steady)

SUMMARY: Ribbons are wrapped loosely around the pole then pulled to spin the crown. Simple and effective: good for all ages and abilities. **This dance requires both sections of the pole to rotate so will not work on every pole.**

This extremely simple dance was taught to Mike by Chris Smith of Maidenhead. It is the only dance we know of that requires both sections of the crown to rotate (achieved by loosening the bolt at the top of the pole) and will not, therefore, work on every pole. However if your pole allows you to do the dance then it works with the very youngest of dancers and breaks the rule about holding ribbons straight. The usual reaction is 'oooh' and 'aaaah' and 'can we do it again?'!

DANCE INSTRUCTIONS

Before you Begin:

- If you have very small dancers, then make sure that there are three or four bigger dancers spaced around the set to ensure that the pattern will unwind successfully.

- All the dancers stand close to the pole, facing to the left, with their ribbons **slack**—*yes really! (Fig. 1)*

Making the Pattern:

1. When the music starts, walk around the pole one or one and a half times;

2. Everyone stop, turn to face the pole and take a firm grip on the ribbons *(Fig. 2)*;

3. All walk back slowly together, pulling evenly on the ribbons;

4. The loose plait will travel upwards and eventually spin the crown around.

Fig. 1: Circling the pole with slack ribbons

Fig. 2: Dancers walk backwards, pulling their ribbons with an even tension

Dance at a Glance

1. All step in and turn left;

2. Loosely wrap ribbons;

3. Pull back to spin crown.

Ribbon Dance Challenges

Once a group of dancers has mastered the basic techniques of Maypole Dancing then there really is no limit as to what can be done. Recent projects have merged street dance with Maypole, horses and land rovers have danced Maypole, and all sorts of patterns from lace making and bell ringing as well as historical dances and ballet have created new ideas. We will be putting links to some of these on the website *(www.themaypolemanual.co.uk)* but here are some challenges that come directly from the dances in the book. We have not given full instructions for two reasons. Firstly, different interpretations might emerge and, secondly, these new dances might feature in a second, advanced Maypole book!

Starting from Barber's Pole:

The Turbine

- Is it possible to have 3 or even 4 concentric circles of dancers at the same time? You might need longer ribbons...

Starting from Chrysanthemum:

How low can you go?!

How many complete patterns can you make down the pole? Taller poles and longer ribbons obviously have an advantage, but you'll be amazed how many layers can be made with even the standard pole.

The Spaghetti Dance

Instead of each colour going the same way around the pole, why not have the second and fourth colours dancing the other way to the first and third? Almost the same dance, but with an attractive variation in pattern.

Starting from The Plaits:

3 in Hand & Runaway Train

We have already mentioned *3 in Hand* as a variation of the *Double Plait*. But Chris Turner has also suggested a more random alternative called *The Runaway Train* where groups of dancers, possibly 3, 4 or even more, weave around while other groups stand still. This is an extension of version 2 of the single plait. Can you make it work as a dance in its own right?

Starting from Easter Plait:

Once everyone has completed a single hey (or plait), then those at the end of the group of three turn around. They should now be facing the outside dancer from the adjacent group. These dancers do a figure called a *back to back*, or *dos-y-do*, with the person facing them, while the middle of each group of three dances in towards the pole and back again. This links the plaits together, making an interesting combination of the *Easter Plait* and *Cobweb*.

Ask the question, 'what would happen if...'

That's how new dances are born...

NON-RIBBON DANCES

Why Maypole dance without ribbons?

For most of us ribbons feature pretty highly on the list of essentials for Maypole Dancing. However here are some reasons why you might include dances without them:

History

The original Maypoles did not have ribbons for dancing. Old pictures and descriptions show that they were much taller than most modern ones as well.

Visual Variety

When the ribbon dances are taking place, people will naturally look at the ribbons. Dancing without ribbons frees dancers to move differently, and gives the audience a fresh focus. As well as circle formations you can have small circles of four people around the pole, or even larger groups spaced around the circle.

Stepping and Phrasing

For many of the ribbon dances, the most important thing is to make sure that the pattern is being made correctly. It can therefore be quite difficult to think about what your feet are doing at the same time. In addition, some of the dances work well to a certain number of beats but not necessarily to phrases of the music. You can change all that with the non-ribbon dances and use them to work on these aspects of dance technique.

Numbers

All the ribbon dances have an obvious restriction on the number of people dancing at any one time. Non-ribbon dances are free from this limitation. So, if you have a class of 30 or more then everyone can join in some of these dances. If you are doing a show, then these dances give a great opportunity for the audience to be involved as well.

Other Traditions

Once we have taken this step away from ribbons, it is then possible to include almost any circular dance from any tradition or culture. Many schools and organisations have done this to make May Day festivities a truly multi-cultural event. You will also find that all sorts of dances can be done both with and without ribbons, maybe with some slight adjustments, which further increases the range of options.

We have included two dances whose origins can be traced back to Victorian England that work particularly well. These are typical of country dances of the period and not very different from many that are still being done at Barn Dances and Ceilidhs around the country. Having tried these, you might want to investigate other dances of this type. Then there are three more from Tudor times. These are genuine dances that may or may not have been danced around a maypole. Use these dances to link to the study of these periods of history.

Practical Considerations

So, dancing without ribbons means one less thing to think about... Or does it?!

Here are some of the extra factors that we haven't encountered before now:

Musical Phrasing

We have touched on aspects of this already but, the music for country dancing is usually in clearly defined phrases. These are usually 4 or 8 bars long, 8 or 16 counts, which are repeated. Therefore, in writing instructions for the dances, we have referred to these phrases as A1, A2, B1 and B2. More details of this can be found in the music section, (p20-21).

Dancing with a Partner

Traditionally each pair comprises a man on the left and a lady to his right. However, all that really matters for these dances is that everyone has a partner and knows who that person is! Depending on your context, you might pair boy with girl, girl with girl, boy with boy, older with younger child, parent with child or simply let the dancers choose their own partner.

Holding Hands

Dancing with ribbons avoids some of the common embarrassment of holding hands with another person! Remember that some dancers may have cultural or religious reasons not to hold hands. For others, it is just unfamiliar and can lead to awkwardness and being silly.

When it comes to non-ribbon dances, giving dancers the choice of who they dance with can help overcome some of the issues. However, we do suggest this with caution - dancers need to take responsibility for their own body weight, and respect the person on the end of their arm, not pulling or dragging each other around!

How to Swing

There are several options for a swing, but we would strongly advise that the best known cross-hand hold is left for experienced dancers as it can be difficult for novices to control. Depending on the age of the dancers, these are good alternatives:

1. Link right arms and turn once around followed by linking left arm *(Fig. 1)*;

2. Jump up and down on the spot, possibly turning around (this is good for very young dancers);

3. Use variations on a ballroom hold (for adults and Victorian authenticity).

Fig 1: Right elbow turn—a good alternative to the traditional swing

CIRCASSIAN CIRCLE

LEVEL: 1   SUGGESTED TRACKS: 14

SUMMARY: A simple circle dance, great for including all your dancers.

The *Circassian Circle* was introduced to England in the mid-nineteenth century. The dance described here was originally called the *Big Set* and was part of that sequence of dances. It is now often used as the final dance of a Barn Dance or Ceilidh. It works particularly well as a finale to a Maypole performance as every dancer can be involved.

Getting Started:

Everyone stands in a large circle with a partner. Traditionally, each pair comprises a man on the left and a lady to his right. However, all that really matters is that everyone knows who their partner is, and who should move when! For ease of terminology, we refer to *Number 1 (#1)* and *Number 2 (#2)*.

Fig. 1: Promenade hold

The Dance:

A1   All hold hands and take 4 steps into the middle and back.

Repeat.

A2   All the #1s take 4 steps in towards the pole, clapping on the 4th beat. Take 4 steps back to place.

#2s do the same.

B1   All swing partners (see *p53* for options and alternatives).

B2   All turn to the right as couples and promenade anti-clockwise around the circle *(Fig. 1)*. With young dancers, don't worry about the hand-hold and just dance in single file instead.

> ## Dance phrases
>
> A1 = 8 bars, or 16 counts
>
> A2 = 8 bars or 16 counts
>
> B1 and B2 the same.
>
> *See p53 for notes on understanding the music*

Thoughts and Tips:

- Encourage dancers to take responsibility for their own body weight, remembering that there is another person attached to the end of their arm!

- *Circassion Circle* can also be used as the basis for a number of ribbon dances—use your imagination...

PAT-A-CAKE POLKA

LEVEL: 1   SUGGESTED TRACKS: 10

SUMMARY: A simple dance that works well in a circle and is great for including all your dancers.

The *Pat-a-cake*, or *'Heel and Toe' Polka*, has been a popular children's dance for many years, probably since the Polka itself was introduced to England in Victorian times and became all the rage. It adapts very well to use around a Maypole, encouraging the dancers to get a greater feel for the rhythm of the music and the shape of the dance.

Getting Started:

In pairs, all dancers stand in a circle, face each other (sideways on to the Maypole) and take a two hand hold.

The Dance:

A1

(4 bars)

(Bars 1 & 2)   With the foot that is nearest the pole tap the heel on the ground and then the toe. Do this twice.

(Bars 3 & 4)   Gallop in towards the pole for 4 steps trying to keep the circle even

A2

(4 bars)

Repeat the heel and toe with the foot furthest from the pole

Gallop back to place

B1

(4 bars)

Clapping with your partner with this suggested sequence:

Right, right, right / left, left, left / both, both, both / knees, knees, knees

B2

(4 bars)

Swing your partner – in the original version, partners would have taken ballroom hold and danced anti-clockwise around the floor or, in this case, the pole.

However the variations of the swing described in Circassian Circle all work well.

Heel (above), toe (right).

THE ARK LARK

LEVEL: 1   SUGGESTED TRACKS: 6

SUMMARY: A simple and slightly silly variation on Pat-a-Cake Polka. A huge favourite with kids of all ages!

This is a modern variant of the traditional *Pat-a-Cake Polka*, learnt from friend and colleague, Alan Simpson. It's a great way for dancers of all ages to let off steam! The dance is exactly the same for the heel and toe, gallops and clapping but, instead of the swing, substitute different animal impressions. A good starting place is for everyone to jump up and down and pretend to be chickens! After that, use your imagination... The main challenges are for the dancers to be ready to start the promenade after 4 bars of this and to listen for each different animal as they are called.

Getting Started:

In pairs, all dancers stand in a circle, face each other (sideways on to the Maypole) and take a two hand hold.

The Dance:

A1 &	Heel and toe & heel and toe; Gallop away from the pole
A2	Heel and toe & heel and toe; Gallop back towards the pole
B1	Clapping with your partner. Use the same sequence as for the Pat-a-Cake Polka or make up a new one.
B2	The leader calls out an animal, and all dancers make impressions!

Tudor Dances

As we have said elsewhere, we do not know exactly which dances the Tudors danced around their Maypoles. What we do know, however, is that they did dance around the Maypole. The dances we describe here were around at the time and they work well when used in this way now.

The first two were originally from France and are called *Brawles* or *Branles* (an old French word meaning to move from side to side or sway – the modern meaning is quite different, and not to be looked up with children!*). They were first written down in a book called *Orchesography* in 1589, although many of the dances were already old. More details can be obtained from the book, now published by Dover. They became extremely popular in the country, although both the spelling and the style often became a *brawl* with people tripping over each other's feet and arguing about it.

There are many different *brawles* and they are quite varied, sometimes just through the steps and sometimes, as featured here, with miming. The music at the time did not always have a regular structure and one of the distinctive features of these dances is that the steps and phrases of the dance and the music were meant to go together.

The third dance, *Sellenger's Round*, was not published until 1670 in the 4th edition of a collection called The Dancing Master by John Playford but it was clearly popular long before that (see the dance notes). It is an excellent example of an early country dance and has survived right through to the present day. It is thought that Queen Elizabeth enjoyed watching the country dances like this when

she went on her Royal Progresses and encouraged her ladies in waiting to dance them for her.

For these Tudor Dances you will need to learn the *Single Step* and the *Double Step*. Both of these can be danced in a number of different ways. They could be incredibly elegant if you were dancing something like a Pavane or a Measure or using a country dance as court entertainment. However, here we are using them as they might have been danced around the Maypole, in other words in the open air on uneven ground where the likelihood is that they would have been kept as simple as possible; so we will do the same.

Stepping

A **Single Step** is just "Step and Close (together)". It can be done forwards, backwards or sideways.

A **Double Step** is "Step, Step, Step and Close (together)". It takes twice as long as a single step and is the basis of many other steps, not only in Tudor times but in all sorts of other styles and traditions. For these dances it is fine just to walk three steps in one direction, turn on the fourth, and take three steps back again.

With very young dancers who find it a challenge to change direction, it can help to extend the step pattern into seven steps before turning around.

---

* Alternative Spellings. We have deliberately chosen a spelling of brawle that does not mean something completely different in another context.

CLOG BRAWLE

LEVEL: 1   SUGGESTED TRACKS: 11

SUMMARY: A simple Tudor dance, one of a series of dances that included an element of mime. Here, everyone pretends that they have clogs (shoes with wooden soles) on their feet.

Getting Started:

All join hands in a circle. Below we have shown you the simplest versions of the steps and arguably the most useful.

The Dance:

A1	Bars 1- 4	Double step to the left (left, right, left together) and a double step to the right,
A2	Bars 5- 8	Repeat A1
B1	Bars 9&10	Single step to the left, Single step to the right,
	Bars 11&12	3 stamps with the right foot,
B2	Bars 13 –16	Repeat B1

Thoughts and Tips:

- Think about posture. How are the dancers holding themselves at the start of the dance before they have even begun to move?

- Starting the dance on the same foot will make it look much smarter.

- Aim for even spacing between dancers and a circle that stays circular!

WASHERWOMAN'S BRAWLE

LEVEL: 2   SUGGESTED TRACKS: 12

SUMMARY: A simple Tudor dance based on the suggestion that all washerwomen were known for liking a good gossip. It offers more opportunities for miming.

All join hands in a large circle. In each couple the dancer on the left is Number 1 and the one on the right Number 2. The dance is done with partners but who dances with who is up to the dancers or the teacher.

A1   Double step to the left and a double step to the right.

A2   Repeat.

   All face your partner.

B1   Number 1s do a single step to the left and one to the right while wagging their finger at their partner - as though making a really important point.

   Meanwhile their partners stand with hands on hips or arms folded. Can your dancers do "attitude"?

B2   Number 2s do same while Number 1s stand still.

C1   All dance 2 single steps left, clapping hands on beats 1 & 3.

   Take 2 single steps to the right, with no clapping.

C2   All dance 2 single steps left, clapping hands on beats 1 & 3.

   All dance 3 spring points, changing weight from one foot to the other while pointing the other foot in front.

Washday painting: Splendoir Solis, c1532, Nuremburg

Thoughts and Tips:

The original description for the dance suggests double steps in the third part, but we have found that doing 2 singles actually helps the dancers to face the middle and get the clapping right. Again, in this context, accurate stepping was probably not a priority.

- Now you have learnt two Tudor dances. Could you use some of the components to create your own dances in this style? What other relevant mime could you include?

SELLENGER'S ROUND

LEVEL: 3   SUGGESTED TRACKS: 13

SUMMARY: One of the most popular country dances that was introduced to court in Tudor times and published over 50 years later during the Period of the Commonwealth.

As with most country dances this is danced with a partner and everyone is in one big circle. Dances of this period usually had a sequence of figures with a chorus after each figure. This is like songs with different verses and then a chorus and we have used this idea in the dance description. The sequence of figures used in this dance was one of the most common sequences used. Nowadays you will see the same sort of figure and chorus construction in many Morris Dances.

Verse 1	**Circle to the left for 8 steps and back to the right.**

This can be walked or done to a slip step with more advanced dancers. (It should really be 2 doubles)

Chorus Facing the middle or the pole:

- **Single Left and Single Right moving forward**
- **Double step back to place**

Facing Partner:

- **Double step back to place**
- **Single Left and Single Right**
- **Turn around to the left using a double step**

Repeat the Chorus

Verse 2 **Siding with Partner**

Face your partner and walk towards them moving slightly to the left so that at the end of a double step you are standing right shoulder to right shoulder. The important thing is to keep your eyes on your partners all the time. Try not to laugh!   Do the same on the other side.

Chorus As above

Verse 3 **Arm Right and Left**

Link your right arm with your partner and walk around in a circle. Repeat with the left arm.

Chorus As above.

Verse 4 **Circling** as in Verse 1.

Chorus As above.

History

In a play called *A Woman Killed with Kindness* written by Thomas Heywood in 1607, a group of rustic characters are arguing about which dance to do and the one they can all agree on is *Sellenger's Round*.

Interestingly the music that everyone now associates with the dance is not that which was originally published in the Dancing Master (1670) but one taken from a set of variations by William Byrd in the Fitzwilliam Virginal Book which was an earlier publication.

TUNES FOR MUSICIANS

Playing for Dancing

In the section that follows you will find music for some of the tunes that Quicksilver play on the accompanying CD (available separately from *www.themaypolemanual.co.uk*). You will notice that what we play is not quite what is written down. This is one thing that makes traditional music very different from classical music. The written music is just the outline of the tune. How any musician plays it will differ slightly: ornamentation and stylistic variations are part of the music. Don't panic, learning the basic tune is where we all started, and the important thing is to become comfortable with that before trying anything too clever.

The idea of including the music is to give a guide to musicians who might want to play for your Maypole Dancing as to the type of tunes we find work well. By having both the written and recorded form we hope that it will encourage musicians to try out some ideas. They may want to add other tunes or to look for something simpler. There are books available for this, but the same rules apply as we gave you for choosing your own recorded music. You will need it to have:

- A strong pulse

- A good tempo

And, above all, to be danceable: certain rhythms will work better for the way your dancers are doing the dances *(p21)*.

Of course you do not have to play tunes like this at all. We often use a solo drum for the *brawles* and many schools have a steel band. Try dancing to their music and watch what it does to the dance. Are there similarities with the dancing that is done in various countries in Central and South America?

Something that we should mention is that, when using live music, it is important for the dancers to know when the music is going start and finish. Agree with your musicians in advance:

- How you will start. Will they give you a count or an introduction?

- How many times through the tune they will play.

- How you will finish the dance. Will the dancers take their cue from the musicians or vice versa?

Of course, with live music you have a lot of flexibility, but thinking ahead to make it work well is the secret of a good show.

Sheet Music: Polkas

Astley's Ride

Trad

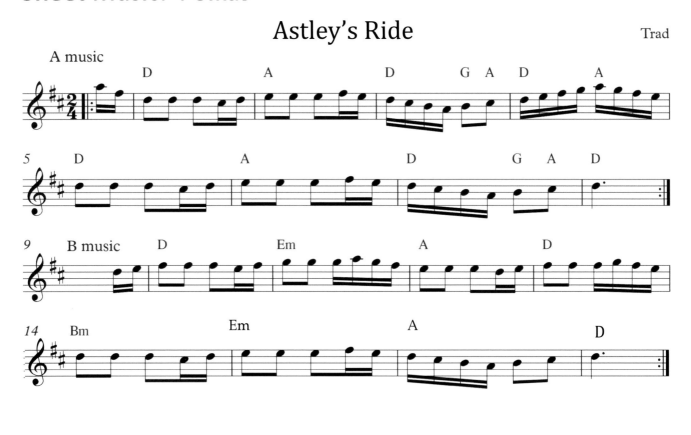

Little Brown Jug

Trad

Mr Cosgill's Delight

Trad

Sheet Music: Jigs and a Polka

The Kesh

Trad

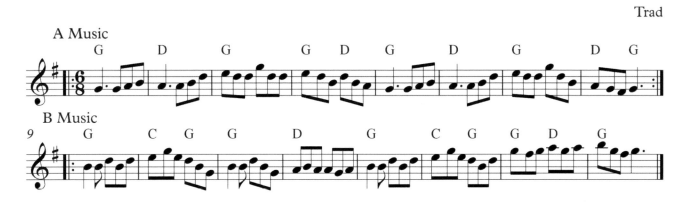

Rakes of Kildare

Trad

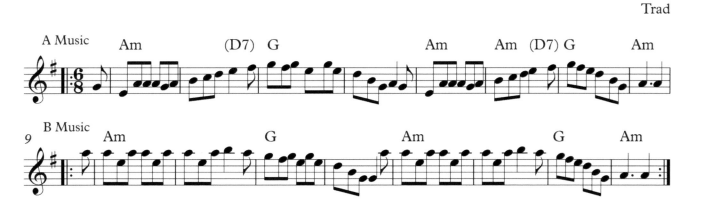

Tralee Gaol

Trad

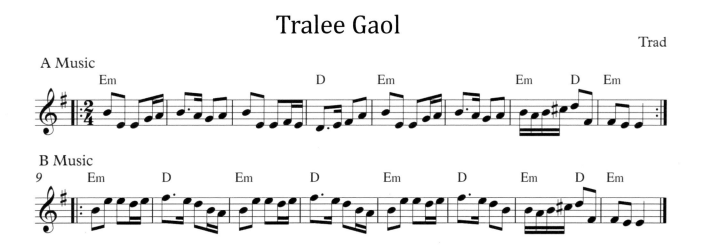

Sheet Music: Tudor Dances

Clog Brawle

Buying a Maypole and Other Resources

Come to us! We have direct contact with Educational Aids, the UK's main supplier of maypoles and accessories, and can sort out any extras that you might need. Find us, the book, the CD and lots of other information about Maypole Dancing, video clips, new dances etc. at *www.themaypolemanual.co.uk* . We will also be able to advise on other resources related to traditional and historical dancing.

You can contact Educational Aids direct at *www.edaids.com* for maypoles at the same price (quote The Maypole Manual) and a wide range of other equipment for schools.

Similarly, both Mike and Jenny have their own organisations offering a range of teaching options for schools, community groups and heritage sites. Mike's is Tradamis with a network of practitioners all around the country *www.tradamis.org* and Jenny's is Spinningpath Arts CIC which is mainly active in the West Country *www.spinningpatharts.org*. We are both used to creating workshops, events and performances from unusual briefs and have links to bands and other groups.

Indoors or outdoors?

Wherever possible, we suggest that teaching is done indoors, particularly for an introductory session. Some of the reasons are:

- Fewer distractions for the dancers
- More stable surface for the Maypole
- Safer surface to dance on
- Easier for the teacher to be heard and greater ability to use sound systems
- The ribbons are much easier to handle without wind and sunshine
- Not affected by cold and rain

All of that being said, sessions can be held outside but the amount being taught will be reduced by the above factors. If you do plan to run sessions and/or performances outside, make sure you have power and a suitably loud sound system available.

What next?

Hopefully you are fully inspired with ideas to make Maypole Dancing your own tradition. But if you still want more ideas, check out our website for dances, suggestions, resources, downloads and more. And if your group have enjoyed Maypole Dancing (which we're sure they will!), then why not explore the many other dance traditions of the British Isles? Morris, social dance, broom dance, clog, step dance, sword dance...

Quick Guide to Dances and Music

Ribbon dances

Page No.	Dance	Level*	Summary	CD Track
26	Circling	1	Simply dancing in a circle around the pole while holding the ribbons.	1,9
28	Barber's Pole	2	A development of Circling, but here the inner and outer circles travel in opposite directions creating two separate spirals.	3, 9
30	Chrysanthemum	1	Flower pattern. Only one colour moves at a time. Good for groups of mixed age and mobility.	2, 6
32	Cobweb	2	Creating a criss-cross pattern or net away from the crown of the pole. Only one colour moves at a time.	8, 10
34	Single Plait	3	Dancers weave a plait around the pole going over and under , similar to a grand chain in country dancing.	2, 3
36	Double Plait	3	Same as Single Plait but travelling with a partner.	2, 7
38	Spiders Web	3	Creates a spider's web effect, with only half the dancers moving at a time.	8, 5
40	Ropes	1	Working in pairs, one person dances around their partner as many times as they can, then then stands still as the partner unwinds it.	7, 9
41	Silkstream	2	Dancers go around and around their partners, twisting the ribbons in pairs. All parade around the pole and back before un-winding.	4 and 5
42	Helter Skelter	4	Asymmetrical pattern created by dancers weaving around the circle, following the lead dancer.	14

Ribbon dances *(contd.)*

Page No.	Dance	Level*	Summary	CD Track
44	Twister	3	1 pair at a time changes place with the person opposite. To unwind, promenade around the pole until the plaits are free, then dance in 2 separate circles.	3, 7
46	Easter Plait	2	Working in groups of 3, the dancers plait their ribbons with the outsides moving to the middle alternately as if plaiting hair.	1, 7
48	Jacobs Ladder	4	In groups of 4 with 2 dancers static, the working couple weave a lattice effect from the pole.	6
50	Water Wheel	1	Effective but very simple. NEEDS BOTH RINGS TO ROTATE. Wrap the ribbons loosely around the pole, then all pull backwards to spin the crown.	5, 4

Non-ribbon dances

Page No.	Dance	Level*	Summary	CD Track
54	Circassian Circle	2	Simple circle dance with partners: includes simple steps, swing and promenade.	1, 6
55	Pat a Cake	1	Simple partner dance: includes simple steps, clapping and swing.	10, 2
56	Ark Lark	2	Simple partner dance: includes simple steps, clapping and animal impressions!	10
58	Clog Brawle	1	Tudor dance with stamping.	11
59	Washerwoman's Brawle	2	Tudor dance with finger wagging.	12
60	Sellenger's Round	3	Tudor country dance in a circle	13

*The dances are rated in order of difficulty, with 1 being the easiest, and 4 the most complex.

References

Books:

Jewitt, Diana (2004). *Dancing Round the Maypole*. London: EFDSS.   Now out of print.

Mason, Sandy (1988). Maypole Dancing. Published privately. Now out of print.

Arbeau, Thoinot (1589). *Orchesography*. Dover Publications. ISBN 10 0486217450 / 13 9780486217451

Images:

Notes for Teachers *(p8-21)*:

1.   Cave painting; *online, source not currently available*

2.   Maypole dancing for the Coronation of George V, 1911; *Rode History website, www.avpu52.dsl.pipex.com/index.html, courtesy of Peter Harris*

3.   St George's Kermis with the dance around the maypole, Pieter Breughel the Younger, 1627; *http://commons.wikimedia.org/wiki/File, oil on panel, Sothebys*

4.   *Microsoft Office Clipart, 2010*

Washerwoman's Brawle *(p59)*:

1.   Washday Painting; *Splendoir Solis, c.1532, Nuremberg, www.oldandinteresting.com/history-of-laundry.aspx*